Debbie Bliss
TIPS FOR KNITTERS

EBURY PRESS · LONDON

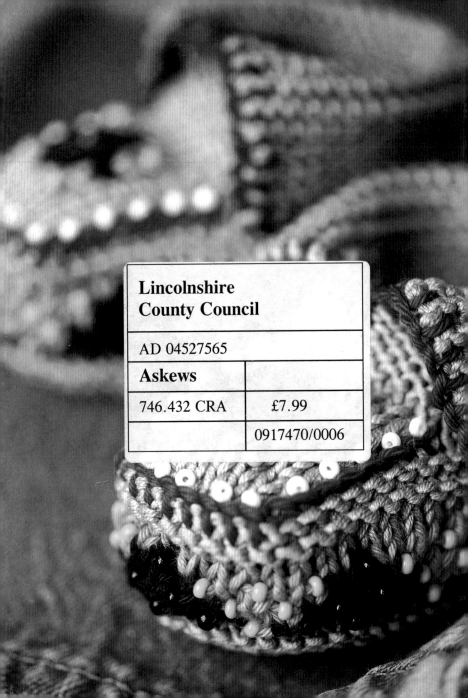

contents

To Mid, my exceptional mother

1 3 5 7 9 10 8 6 4 2

Published in 2009 by Ebury Press, an imprint of Ebury Publishing

A Random House Group Company

The Random House Group Limited Reg. No. 954009

Addresses for companies within the Random House Group can be
found at www.randomhouse.co.uk

A CIP catalogue record for this book is available from the British Library

The Random House Group Limited supports The Forest Stewardship
Council (FSC), the leading international forest certification organisation.
All our titles that are printed on Greenpeace-approved FSC-certified
paper carry the FSC logo. Our paper procurement policy can be found
at www.rbooks.co.uk/environment

To buy books by your favourite authors and register for offers visit
www.rbooks.co.uk

Printed and bound in Malaysia by Tien Wah Press

ISBN 9780091927615

Editor: Emma Callery
Designer: Isobel Gillan
Photography: Sandra Lane and Sandra Lousada
Stylist: Sammie Bell
Illustrations: Kate Simunek
Charts and diagrams: Antony Duke

Introduction

This handy little book of tips and hints is aimed at both new knitters who want a quick reference guide to the basics of the craft, and the more experienced knitters who want to improve their techniques and begin to create their own ideas. It is just the right size to carry around with your projects and dip into when you need to clarify a technique or better understand a pattern.

From simple shaping to creating textures, to adding embroidery to your garments, working edgings or incorporating buttons and beads, this book will help you broaden your knitting skills and give you some ideas for creating your own unique looks.

Debbie Bliss

YARNS

From rustic tweeds to crisp
cottons and sensuous silks,
there is a wonderful range
of fibres to choose from now.
With classic and fancy yarns, smooth
and slub, there are yarns to suit every
season, look or mood. With such great choice
and with new yarns coming out every year, it can
be difficult to know which to use. The following pages
may help you decide.

yarn fibres

Fibres are divided into two main categories: natural and synthetic.

- Natural fibres are then divided into animal fibres – wool, angora, cashmere, silk – and those from vegetable fibres, such as cotton, linen and hemp.

- Synthetic fibres are made from polyester, nylon and acrylic. Synthetic fibres tend to get a bad press – and for good reason. Although they are cheaper and can be thrown into a washing machine, they don't have the same insulating properties as natural fibres and can produce a limp, flat fabric that will melt on contact with an iron.

- When synthetic fibres are blended with natural yarns, they can add durability and lightness.

- My preference is to use, where possible, natural fibres or those containing a small amount of man-made fibres.

types of yarn

Wool

Wool, spun from the fleece of sheep, is the yarn that is most commonly associated with knitting. It has many excellent properties as it is durable, elastic, and warm in winter.

- Wool yarn is particularly good for working colour patterns, since the fibres adhere together and help prevent Fair Isle or intarsia patterns from 'pulling away' and forming gaps.

- Some knitters also find that simple stitch patterns, such as garter stitch and moss (seed) stitch, can look neater and the knitted fabric more even, in a wool rather than a cotton yarn.

- Superwash wool has been treated to allow for machine washing.

Cotton

Cotton yarn, made from a natural plant fibre, is warm in the winter and cool in the summer, making it an ideal all-seasons fibre. It is a good yarn to use when there is subtle stitch detailing, as the crispness of the yarn adds clarity to the stitch.

- Make sure you use a really good-quality cotton for the knitted cotton fabric; if it has been worked in a poorer-quality cotton, it can droop and lose its elasticity after washing, particularly on ribbed borders.

Knitting yarn that is made from a blend of wool and cotton fibres is particularly good for children's knitwear. This is because the wool content gives elasticity for comfort, and the cotton content is perfect for those children who find wool fibres scratchy and irritating on the skin.

Alpaca

Often as soft as cashmere, alpaca yarn is a cheaper alternative. Made from an animal related to the llama, it is hardwearing and resistant to pilling.

Bamboo

A very silky yarn that drapes beautifully.

Camel

Made from the Bactrian camel, it is soft but rather un-elastic, so it is often better combined with wool.

Cashmere

Made from the underhair of a particular Asian goat, cashmere yarn will always be seen as the ultimate in luxury. It is absolutely beautiful and unbelievably soft to the touch. It can be expensive due to the shortage of supply, but if you find the cost prohibitive, try using it for small items such as scarves or baby clothes.

Linen

Made from the flax plant, linen yarn is one of the earliest fibres used by man in textiles. It is beautiful in classic, simple shapes, but can be rather hard to the touch in hand-knitting yarn.

Organic yarns

Made from fibre that is produced without the use of man-made chemicals, such as herbicides, pesticides or chemical fertiliser.

Rayon

Made from the cellulose of wood pulp, this is a natural fibre that is treated chemically.

Silk

Silk is a fibre produced by silk moths as they spin their cocoons. Its beauty can make up for some of its less practical properties, as it can be inclined to pill and is not a very elastic yarn.

plies and weights

Yarn is made up from one or more strands of fibre called plies, several of which are twisted together to form 'plied yarn'. The thickness of yarn comes not from the number of plies, but the individual thickness of each ply. For example, a yarn with four plies can be finer than a single-ply bulky yarn.

- Yarns come in different weights of thicknesses and range from fine 2- or 3-ply yarns to bulky, chunky yarns. The thickness of the yarn determines how many stitches and rows there are to 2.5 cm (1 in) and is the basis on which all knitting patterns are created.

- Yarns with a tight twist are usually strong and smooth, and those with a looser twist are generally softer and less even. They can pull apart if over-handled and may not be suitable for sewing up your garment.

most commonly used yarns

The following yarns are those that are most frequently used in commercial knitting patterns and are readily available.

- **Aran weight:** Slightly thicker than a DK (see double knitting, below) and traditionally used in Aran or fishermen's sweaters, Aran is knitted on 4.5 mm (US 7) or 5 mm (US 8) needles. The tension is usually 18 sts to 10 cm (4 in). For example, Debbie Bliss Rialto Aran.

- **Chunky:** Knitted on 6.5 mm (US 10.5) needles, the tension is usually 14 sts to 10 cm (4 in). For example, Debbie Bliss Cashmerino Chunky.

- **Double knitting:** Often referred to as DK, this yarn is knitted on 4 mm (US 6) needles. The tension is usually 22 sts to 10 cm (4 in). For example, Debbie Bliss Rialto Double Knitting.

- **4-ply:** A fine yarn knitted on 3.25 mm (US 3) needles. The tension is usually 28 sts to 10 cm (4 in). For example, Debbie Bliss Rialto 4-ply.

- **Lightweight yarn:** This is a yarn that is slightly thicker than a 4-ply and is worked on the same-sized needles. It is between a 4-ply and a double knitting yarn. The tension is usually 25 sts to 10 cm (4 in). For example, Debbie Bliss Baby Cashmerino.

other yarn descriptions

You may come across these technical terms when choosing yarn:

- **Blends:** Yarns made from a mix of fibres, such as wool/cotton, cotton/silk. They can often combine the best of both worlds; for instance, the elasticity of wool with the coolness of cotton.

- **Fancy or novelty yarns:** These yarns tend to be part of a fashion trend for a particular season. They are often textured, such as the curly looking bouclé, or maybe a shiny ribbon yarn. They do not always have a very long shelf-life, so knit it while you can, or if it is for a project that you are going to put on the back burner, make sure you have enough yarn!

- **Felted yarns:** These have been treated so that when knitted they give the soft and fuzzy appearance of felted fabric.

- **Heathers:** Yarns that combine grey fleece yarn with dyed yarns, giving a soft, muted look.

- **Marls:** Yarns of two or more plies where the plies are different colours.

- **Random or variegated yarns:** These have been dyed with different shades along the length of the yarn. They can be a good way of achieving colour effects without having to change yarn and colours.

- **Roving:** Yarns that are unspun and loosely plied. When pulled, they break easily, but when knitted, they make very soft garments.

- **Slub:** These have a textured appearance with 'clumps' on the surface. Achieved by combining a smooth yarn as the core with an outer, uneven ply.

- **Smooth:** These tend to be the yarns with the tighter twist. They are sometimes also referred to as classic yarns. The smooth surface makes them perfect for showing up stitches, which is particularly important with subtle stitch patterns or cables.

- **Tweeds:** Yarns with a background shade contrasting with flecks of different colours.

buying yarn for a knitting pattern

Make every effort to buy the yarn specified in the pattern. The designer will have created the design with that yarn in mind and a substitute may produce a garment that is different from the one that you had wanted to make. For instance, a design's appeal may rely on a subtle stitch pattern, which is lost when using a yarn of inferior quality.

- If you do substitute the yarn and use a synthetic yarn instead of a natural fibre, or even wool where cotton had been originally used, the stitch patterns may appear softer and less delineated. Synthetics can also appear limp, which means that the crispness of the original garment will have been lost.

- No manufacturer will accept responsibility for problems you may have with the sizing of a pattern or with wash and wear if a different yarn has been used.

- It is essential to check metreage or yardage. The fibre content and make up of the yarn determine how much yarn you get for the weight. In other words, two 50 g (1¾ oz) balls may have different lengths of yarn, so you may need to buy more or less yarn than the quantity quoted in the pattern.

- If you do decide to substitute a yarn, buy one that is the same weight and, where possible, the same fibre content. It is essential to use a yarn that has the same tension or your measurements will be different from the original design. The garment will have been designed to specific proportions and a difference in tension may mean the boxy sweater you fell in love with has become a skinny tunic.

- Check the ball band on the yarn (see overleaf).

understanding ball bands

By checking the ball band on the yarn you will have nearly all the information you need before you start your project.

- **Yarn weight:** The company's name and brand name will tell you whether you have the right yarn for the design. Check carefully as there may be different weights of yarn within the same named range. For example, in my Cashmerino range there is a lightweight DK, a DK, an aran and a chunky weight. The tension and needles quoted on the band will also help you here. A standard double knitting weight is usually 22 sts to 10 cm (4 in) and knitted on 4 mm (US 6) needles. An aran weight is usually 18 sts and knitted on 4.5 mm (US 7) needles.

- **The metreage or yardage:** The length will inform you as to whether you need to buy fewer or more balls if you are substituting a yarn. The weight will tell you in grammes or ounces the weight of the ball. It is also important to check this if you are not using the yarn quoted. It is all too easy to buy, for example, eight 50 g (1³⁄₄ oz) balls and then on rereading the pattern realise the original yarn was in 100 g (4 oz) balls and you should have bought double the amount.

- **Fibre content:** This will tell you, for example, whether the yarn is cotton, wool, acrylic or a blend, and care instructions will let you know whether the finished garment should be hand-washed, machine-washed or dry-cleaned.

- **Dye lot number:** Check this because yarns are dyed in batches or lots, and the colour can sometimes vary considerably. Your retailer may not have the same dye lot later, so try to buy all your yarn for your project at the same time. If you know that sometimes you use more yarn than is quoted in the pattern, buy more yarn initially. If it is not possible to buy all the yarn you need with the same dye lot, work the borders, such as cuffs, ribs or collar, in the odd lot, as it is less likely to show.

EQUIPMENT

The first-time knitter needs only the most basic pieces of equipment to start with. Some are essential, such as knitting needles, scissors, tape measure and darning needle. Others are helpful, such as row counters and a needle gauge. At the beginning of a pattern it will list all the items you need to start your project.

knitting needles

Knitting needles come in a range of materials, sizes, styles and prices. As you progress, you will begin to use the type of needles that suit you best.

- Knitting needles have been around for a very long time and have been made in a variety of materials from ivory to whalebone. Since they were first mass produced in steel they have been made in wood, aluminium, plastic and more.

- For beginners, I would recommend bamboo needles, as they have a silky finish that lets the stitches glide across the needle. They are good for clammy hands – one of the disadvantages of the new, nervous knitter! Bamboo needles also prevent you from knitting too quickly – another plus point for the beginner.

There are three types of needle: straight, double pointed, and circular.

- Straight knitting needles are sold in pairs and come in three lengths. There is a knob at one end to prevent your stitches falling off the needle. You will need longer needles for work that is wider or if you need to pick up a lot of stitches – for instance, down the front edges of a jacket. A pattern should tell you if you need to use longer needles.

- Double-pointed needles have a point at each end and come in sets of four or five needles. They are only ever used for circular knitting and usually over a small amount of stitches, such as when making socks, mittens or hats.

- Circular needles are usually used for circular knitting when there is no seam. They have a working point at each end of a flexible nylon wire and are useful when for a large number of stitches, such as on a blanket or afghan, when you can use them working backwards and forwards.

needle conversion chart

This needle conversion chart covers all the most frequently used knitting needle sizes. A needle's size is determined by its diameter; the smaller the needle, the smaller the size of the stitch, and vice versa. Finer yarns are worked on smaller needles and bulkier yarns on larger ones.

• If you are not able to achieve the tension or number of stitches and rows to 10 cm (4 in) that the pattern states, you will need to change your needle size to obtain the size of stitch required (see Tension on page 54).

METRIC	US SIZES
2 mm	0
2.25 mm	1
2.75 mm	2
3 mm	2/3
3.25 mm	3
3.5 mm	4
3.75 mm	5
4 mm	6
4.5 mm	7
5 mm	8
5.5 mm	9
6 mm	10
6.5 mm	10.5
7 mm	10.5
7.5 mm	11
8 mm	11
9 mm	13
10 mm	15

other tools

There are a few other tools that are essential to have to hand before you start to knit.

- **Darning needle:** Use a blunt tipped darning or tapestry needle to sew up seams once you've finished knitting.

- **Row counter:** This fits on the end of your needle so that you can check row numbers. It's not essential, but it is helpful.

- **Safety pins:** Use these as mini stitch holders or to mark where you have made increases on a sleeve, for example.

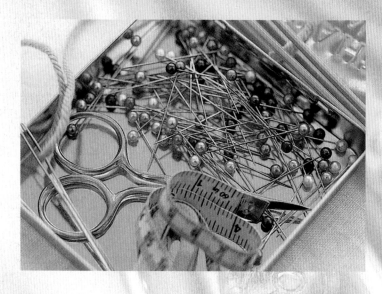

- **Scissors:** These are important as they save you from the temptation of breaking off yarn with your teeth! A pair of small scissors with sharp points is best, preferably with a case if you are going to be carrying them around with your knitting.

- **Stitch holder:** You will need one of these to secure stitches, such as at a front neck, that you are going to work later.

- **Tape measure or ruler:** As you progress from practice squares, you will also need a tape measure or ruler marked with centimetres and inches to measure your tension square and your knitted pieces.

UNDERSTANDING PATTERNS

Most patterns adhere to a fairly recognisable structure. They will tell you what yarn to use, how much of it to buy, and needle sizes, measurements, tension and abbreviations. First of all, check that the pattern suits your capabilities. If you are a beginner, choose a design that is fairly simple or you may be disheartened to find yourself struggling with techniques and stitch patterns that you are not quite ready to tackle.

before you begin

I used to tell knitters to read the pattern carefully first, but I am changing my views on this as I feel that some parts of the pattern, which are simple and make sense when you are actually knitting them, seem confusing when reading through initially. Some instructions only really make sense when the knitting is on the knitting needles.

- However, do read the materials list before you leave the shop with your pattern and yarn. Check the equipment you need carefully. There is nothing worse than getting home, eager to start your project, only to find that you assumed that a certain weight of yarn required the most obvious needle size and that for that particular pattern you need needles you do not have, or that a cable needle was required.

- Check for additional materials that you may need, such as a zipper, etc. Buttons are sometimes best left to be chosen after the garment has been finished, to get a sense of size and the most appropriate design.

- Look at the measurements on the knitting instructions before buying yarn, to be sure which size garment that you want to knit. Most patterns quote the actual finished knitted size rather than just the bust/chest measurements of the wearer. The actual measurements will tell you the width around the whole garment, which, in turn, tells you how much ease a garment has, whether it is a generous, baggy style or slim fitting.

- If you wish to make up the design with less or more ease, you may just need to knit the smaller or larger size quoted. If you are unsure, measure an existing garment you have, to compare. The length of the garment is usually taken from the shoulder shaping to the cast-on edge.

- Make every effort to use the yarn that has been recommended in the pattern. This yarn will have been tried and tested in the sample garment, and the designer will have worked with it because it produces the best possible look for the design. (For more about buying yarn for your knitting, see pages 26–7).

understanding instructions

For a beginner, knitting pattern instructions can look indecipherable, but, just as when learning a new language, what at first seems baffling will soon become familiar to you.

- If you are working a pattern from a book of designs you may find it helpful to photocopy the pattern so that you can carry it around without damaging the original, especially if you knit 'on the go'! This will also give you the opportunity to highlight the size you are making, if you need to, and jot down notes and mark where you are if you need to leave your project for a time.

- When working a jacket or cardigan where you have two front pieces, remember that the Right Front refers to the right front as you are wearing it rather than as you are looking at it.

- Work the instructions given in square brackets the number of times stated. Where 0 appears, no stitches or rows are worked for this size. Many queries I have from knitters regarding stitch counts are due to misreading brackets.

- Asterisks are also used to indicate a repeat, as in * k1, p1, rep from * twice. When two parts of a garment share the same instructions, asterisks are also used, as in rep from * to **. This means repeat the instructions between the asterisks.

- There is rarely space in a knitting pattern to write out all the instructions in full. For this reason, abbreviations are sometimes used throughout the pattern. These will be explained in full before the pattern starts – or, in the case of a book, on a page dedicated to abbreviations (see page 47).

- Schematics or diagrams are often given with a pattern. These are helpful as they show the shape of the finished pieces and their measurements.

pattern sizes

Most patterns – depending on the style – are written for a range of garment sizes. The smallest size is given first in the instructions and appears outside the round brackets (or parentheses); the larger sizes are given inside the brackets.

* Make sure, as you follow the pattern, that you are consistently using the right stitches for your size – it is only too easy to switch sizes inside the brackets. One way to avoid this is to go through the instructions first and mark the size you are knitting with a coloured pen or highlighter.

* If you are unsure of the size you want to knit, it can be helpful to measure a garment of a similar style that you have and compare the measurements. This may guide you in deciding whether you want to knit, for example, the 81/86 cm (32/34 in) or the 86/92 cm (34/36 in) bust size. It is particularly useful when you are knitting for a child and the pattern is given in ages. The ages are only a general aid, as children come in all shapes and sizes, of course, and tend to grow in length rather than width, but if you measure an existing garment that they wear comfortably, that will give you a good start in choosing the right size. Remember that you should also allow for the child's growth.

- If you want to alter the measurements of a pattern, make sure that there isn't a good reason why the size you want has been left out! It may be that the design doesn't translate well in all sizes and that it would need a complete redesign in order to make it work. To accommodate a large stitch repeat, the sizes offered may have been restricted and by adding the stitches or rows you need for the width or length you want, you could be starting or ending the garment in an unattractive part of the pattern.

- If you want to alter a pattern that you like, and it is a simple one with a small or no pattern repeat, check the tension to see how many stitches and rows there are to 1 cm ($\frac{1}{2}$ in). Add or subtract the number of stitches or rows that you need to alter the width or length before working the armhole shaping. If there is shaping at the sides, you will need to re-calculate the increasings or decreasings over the changed number of rows.

- When changing the stitch count, remember that this will alter the number of stitches you have at the shoulders and neck shaping.

abbreviations

Knitting terms are frequently written out in an abbreviated form and so can seem unfamiliar. The list below includes the abbreviations that are most frequently used. If a knitting pattern has more specific abbreviations, they are usually explained at the beginning of the pattern.

A, B, C, D = contrasting colours
approx = approximately
alt = alternate
beg = begin(ning)
cont = continu(e)(ing)
cm = centimetre(s)
cn = cable needle
dec = decreas(e)(ing)
DK = double knitting
foll = follow(ing)
g = gram(mes)
in = inch(es)
inc = increas(e)(ing)
inc 1 = increase one stitch by working into the front and back of the stitch
k = knit
k2tog = knit two together
m1 = make one by picking up the loop lying between the stitch just worked and the next stitch and working into the back of it

mb = make bobble
mm = millimetre(s)
oz = ounce(s)
patt = pattern
p = purl
psso = pass slipped stitch over
rem = remain(ing)
rep = repeat(ing)
RS = right side
skpo = slip one, knit one, pass slipped stitch over
sl = slip
ssk = slip, slip, knit
st(s) = stitch(es)
st st = stocking stitch
tbl = through back of loop(s)
tog = together
WS = wrong side
yb = yarn back
yf = yarn forward
yon = yarn over needle
yrn = yarn around needle

frequently used knitting terms

On this page and overleaf, are the commonly used terms that you will find in knitting patterns.

along neck = this is usually used when picking up stitches around the straight edge of a neck.

around neck = this is usually used when picking up stitches around the curved edge of a neck.

as folls = work the instructions as they follow.

at the same time = work the instructions that follow at the same time as those that immediately preceded it. Often occurs when you start shaping a neckline at the same time as working armhole shaping.

each end = usually used when shaping. Work at both the beginning and the end of the row.

easing in any fullness = usually used at the top of a sleeve head or when sewing on a collar or hood. It indicates you need to gather the extra fullness into the seam.

ending with a WS (RS) row = the last row is a wrong-side (right-side) row.

from beg = used when you need to know the measurement of the piece. Take the measurement from the cast-on edge, unless otherwise stated.

increase stitches evenly across row = this normally appears after a rib row when extra stitches are required.

inc. sts into patt. = as you increase, work the extra stitches into the established pattern.

pick up and k = usually used when picking up stitches around a neck or edge by pulling up loops through the stitches and rows of an edge.

place markers = place a stitch marker or contrast piece of yarn at each end of a row. Often used to indicate a place from which a measurement will be taken.

reversing shaping = usually found on neck shaping or when working the fronts of cardigans where the instructions will be the same but reversed. For example, on neck shaping the first side will be worked first, then the second side as in 'work as on first side, reversing shapings'. When reversing shaping, it is neater if you also reverse the way the stitches slope, so on the left side neck you would work k2tog at the neck edge, but on the other side skpo or ssk.

same as = follow instructions given for another piece of the garment.

slip sts onto a holder = transfer those stitches onto a stitch holder.

turning = switching your knitting from the right side to the wrong side, or vice versa. Turning rows are when the work is turned before completing the row so that extra rows are worked within a row. Usually seen in sock or collar shaping.

with RS facing = the right side of the work should be facing you.

with WS facing = the wrong side of the work should be facing you.

working in patt = continue to follow the pattern.

uk and us terminology

Knitting terminology varies between the UK and US. Here is a list of those expressions that are most frequently used.

UK TERM	US TERM
Aran wool	'fisherman' yarn
ball band	yarn wrapper or label
brackets, round	parentheses
brackets, square	brackets
cast off	bind off
DK (double knitting)	a yarn weight between sport and worsted
double moss stitch	double seed stitch
every alternate row	every other row
make up	finish
moss stitch	seed stitch
stocking stitch	stockinette stitch
tension	gauge
welt	lower borders on sweater front and back
yf	yarn over (yo), or yarn to front of work between two needles
yon, yrn	yarn over (yo)

tension/gauge

It is crucial to check your tension before you embark on any project. 'Tension' is the number of stitches and rows to a centimetre or inch and is also known as 'stitch gauge' or simply 'gauge'. The tension determines the measurements of a garment, so it is very important that you obtain the same number of rows and stitches as the designer.

- A small difference over 10 cm (4 in) can add up to a considerable amount over the complete width of the knitted garment. If your tension is looser or tighter than the one stated in the knitting pattern, your garment will be larger or smaller than the original garment. So taking time out for 15 minutes to work a tension square before you start can save a lot of disappointment later on.

- The size of the stitch depends on the yarn, the size of the knitting needles and your control of the yarn. It can also depend on mood – many knitters will have experienced a tighter tension when stress levels are higher!

- I prefer to let my swatch 'settle' for a few hours before I measure it so that the stitches and rows have relaxed, giving a more accurate count.

- To work out the tension, use the same yarn and needles and stitch pattern that the tension has been measured over in the pattern, and knit a sample at least 13 cm (5¹/₂ in) square. Then smooth out the square on a flat surface.

- To check stitch tension, place a ruler (a cloth tape measure can be less accurate) horizontally on the fabric and mark 10 cm (4 in) with pins. Count the number of stitches between the pins.

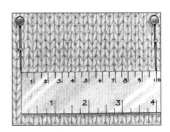

- To check row tension, place a ruler vertically, mark 10 cm (4 in) with pins and count the number of rows.

- If the number of stitches and rows is greater than it says in the pattern, your tension is tighter. This can usually be regulated by using larger needles. If the number of stitches is fewer than the specified number, your tension is looser and you should change to smaller needles. Your tension may change from that of your sample when knitting the actual garment, as your knitting can alter when working across more stitches.

- It can be more difficult to count rows on garter stitch as every second row is hidden. Count each horizontal ridge as two rows.

BEGINNING TO KNIT

The first step when beginning to knit is to cast on. There are several ways of doing this, but there are two cast-on methods – the thumb and the cable – that seem to be the most frequently used. The best one to choose is the one that you feel most comfortable with, or that produces the kind of edge you prefer. You may choose to use a different cast-on technique depending on where you will be using it on the garment. The cable cast on, for example, produces a firm edge that can be useful in an area that may get a lot of wear, such as on sleeve cuffs.

casting on

Before learning how to cast on, check that you are holding your needles correctly. Some knitters hold their right needle like a pen, some like a knife. I prefer to knit in the 'pen' style as I find it helps me knit more quickly and more fluently. Try this first, as illustrated below, and then try holding it over the needle and see which you feel more comfortable with.

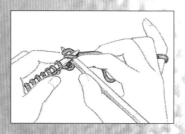

◁ Holding needles
To hold the yarn in your right hand, pass it around your little finger, under your centre finger and over your index finger. Your index finger is used to pass the yarn around the tip of the needle. The yarn circled around your little finger creates the necessary tension for even knitting.

Starting with a slip knot

To start most cast-on methods, you first need to make a simple slip knot, also called a 'slip loop'. This makes the slip knot the very first 'stitch' that you cast on your knitting needle. To make it clear which end of the yarn comes from the yarn ball, the loose end is shown short so it fits in the diagram, but in reality you should leave a long loose end so it can either be darned in or used to sew the seam.

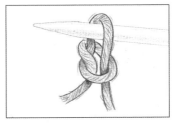

1 Wind the yarn twice around the fingers on your left hand to make a circle of yarn, as shown in the inset. With the knitting needle, pull a loop of the yarn attached to the ball through the yarn circle on your fingers.

2 Then pull both ends of the yarn to tighten the slip knot onto the knitting needle. You are now ready to use one of the following cast-on methods to cast stitches onto your knitting needle (see pages 60–7).

thumb cast on

I use the thumb cast-on method (see page 63), because as a fairly tight knitter I find it gives me a fast, fluid cast on with an edge that I like. It has quite a bit of 'give' in it, which makes it ideal for edges that need some flexibility and stretch, for instance on the roll-up brim of a beanie hat.

- One word of warning with the thumb cast-on method – because you are casting on and working towards the end of the yarn (unlike two-needle methods where you work towards the ball), you have to predict how much yarn is needed for the amount of stitches required. You may find that you are left with a few more stitches to make and not enough yarn to make them with. Depending on the thickness of the yarn, 1 m (39 in) creates about 100 stitches.

- If you are unsure how much yarn you will need, over-compensate by allowing more yarn. You can then always use the extra length to sew up the seams.

- Generally, knitters are taught to use a slip knot to begin with when casting on with this method. However, once you become confident with the technique, rather than use a slip knot, work the first stitch by simply laying the yarn over your thumb from front to back and holding the yarn as before with the yarn over the right needle – then knit into the thumb loop. I find that this gives a slightly neater edge.

To work the English thumb cast on

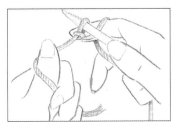

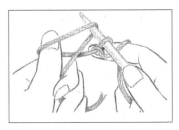

1 Make a slip knot as shown on page 59, leaving a long tail. With the slip knot on the needle in your right hand and the yarn that comes from the ball over your index finger, wrap the tail end of the yarn over your left thumb from front to back, securing the yarn in your palm with your fingers.

2 Then insert the knitting needle upwards through the yarn loop on your left thumb.

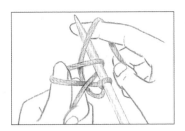

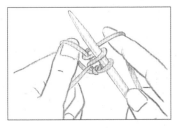

3 Next, with the right index finger, wrap the yarn from the ball up and over the point of the knitting needle.

4 Then draw the yarn through the loop on your thumb to form a new stitch on the knitting needle. Lastly, let the yarn loop slip off your left thumb and pull the loose end to tighten up the stitch. Repeat these steps to make the stitches you need.

To work the European thumb cast on

This cast on is worked in the same way as the English thumb cast on, except that both ends of the yarn are held in the left hand. Because knitters on the continent usually knit with the working yarn held in their left hand, they generally prefer this type of thumb cast on over the 'English' method. As explained on the previous page, you can do without the slip knot if you prefer.

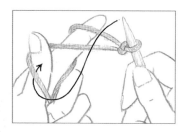

1 Hold the needle with the slip knot in your right hand and the tail end of the yarn in your left hand, as for the English method, but put the yarn from the ball over the left index finger and secure both ends in your palm with your fingers. To begin, insert the knitting needle through the thumb loop, as shown by the arrow.

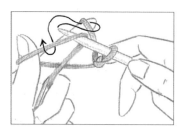

2 'Grab' the yarn on the index finger with the knitting needle, as shown by the arrow, and pull a loop through the loop on the thumb.

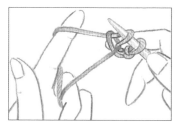

3 Let the yarn loop slip off your left thumb and pull both ends to tighten up the new cast-on stitch. Continue casting on in this way until you have the stitches you need.

- On reversible fabrics, after casting on you can decide which is the wrong side of the fabric. You can then check this by noticing whether the 'tail' of your cast-on yarn is on the left- or right-hand side of the work. With the thumb cast on, this tail will be at the opposite end of the work to the cable cast on (see page 66). (Although your fabric is reversible, you will need to know which is the right side and which the wrong side when working shaping, etc.)

cable cast on

The cable cast on is a popular method of casting on that creates a firm edge. It can be a good cast on to use where an elastic, but sturdier, foundation row would be an advantage. Those with a standard-to-tight tension, like myself, may find it more difficult to insert the knitting needle between the stitches and pull the yarn through, so make sure that you do not tighten up each new stitch on the left-hand needle too much. (See more about your knitting tension on pages 54–5.)

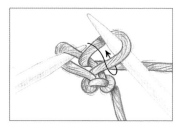

1 Make a slip knot, as shown on page 59. Then hold the knitting needle with the slip knot in your left hand and insert the right-hand needle from left to right and from front to back through the slip knot. Wrap the yarn from the ball up and over the point of the right-hand needle, as shown.

2 With the right-hand needle, draw a loop through the slip knot to make a new stitch. Do not drop the stitch from the left-hand needle, but instead slip the new stitch onto the left-hand needle, as shown.

3 Then insert the right-hand needle between the two stitches on the left-hand needle and wrap the yarn around the point of the right-hand needle.

4 Pull the yarn through to make a new stitch, and then place the new stitch onto the left-hand needle, as before. Repeat the last two steps to make the stitches you need.

THE STITCHES

After casting on stitches, you knit or purl them according to what your knitting pattern requires. Though the basic techniques for making knit or purl stitches are very simple, they are what builds up the whole knitted fabric.

the knit stitch

The knit stitch is the very first stitch you will learn and forms a reversible fabric called garter stitch (see the scarf opposite). Follow the three steps below to make the knit stitch. When you have worked all the stitches from the left-hand needle onto the right-hand needle, you have completed a 'row'. You then turn the work, transferring the needle with all the stitches to the left-hand, and continue as before.

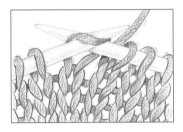

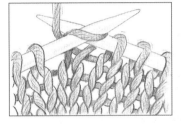

1 With the cast-on stitches on the needle in your left hand, insert the right-hand needle from left to right and from front to back through the first cast-on stitch.

2 Then take the yarn from the ball on your index finger (the working yarn) around the point of the right-hand needle.

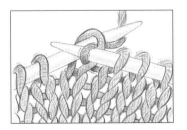

3 Draw the right-hand needle and yarn through the stitch, thus forming a new stitch on the right-hand needle and, at the same time, slip the original stitch off the left-hand needle. Repeat these steps until all the stitches from the left-hand needle have been worked. This is called a row.

the purl stitch

After the knit stitch, the next stitch to discover is the purl stitch. This is the reverse of the knit stitch, but if every row is worked as a purl row it creates the same fabric as if you had knitted every row – garter stitch (see page 78). By alternating purl rows with knit rows, you create stocking stitch (see the beanie hat opposite and page 79). When working stocking stitch, try to keep your tension consistent on both your knit and purl rows.

1 With the yarn to the front of the work, insert the right-hand needle from right to left into the front of the first stitch on the left-hand needle.

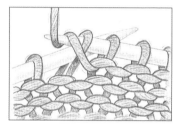

2 Then take the yarn from the ball on your index finger (the working yarn) around the point of the right-hand needle.

3 Draw the right-hand needle and the yarn through the stitch, thus forming a new stitch on the right-hand needle, and at the same time slip the original stitch off the left-hand needle. Repeat these steps until all the stitches have been worked.

casting off

Casting off is the method used after you have completed your knitting to secure the stitches so they do not unravel. It is important that the cast-off edge is neither too tight nor too loose, and that it is elastic. This is particularly important when casting off on a neckband so that it can be pulled easily over the head.

- Casting off is also used to make some types of buttonholes and when more than one stitch needs to be decreased at once.

- Unless otherwise stated, cast off in the stitch pattern being used on the garment.

Knit cast off

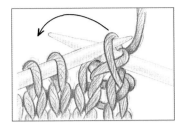

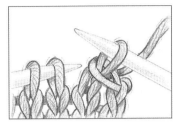

1 Knit two stitches. Then * insert the left-hand needle into the first stitch knitted on the right-hand needle and lift this stitch over the second stitch and off the right-hand needle.

2 One stitch is now on the right-hand needle. Knit the next stitch. Repeat the first step from * until all the stitches have been cast off. Then pull the yarn through the last stitch to fasten off.

Purl cast off

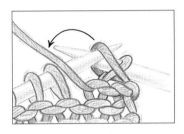

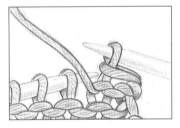

1 Purl two stitches. * Insert the left-hand needle into the back of the first stitch worked on the right-hand needle and lift this stitch over the second stitch and off the right-hand needle.

2 One stitch is now on the right-hand needle. Purl the next stitch. Repeat the first step from * until all the stitches have been cast off. Then pull the yarn through the last stitch to fasten off.

combining stitches

By combining knit and purl stitches in various ways, many different knitted textures can be created. The most basic textures and the ones used the most frequently are garter stitch and stocking stitch (see pages 78 and 79), reverse stocking stitch and double ribbing (see pages 80 and 81) and moss (seed) stitch and double moss stitch (see pages 82 and 83).

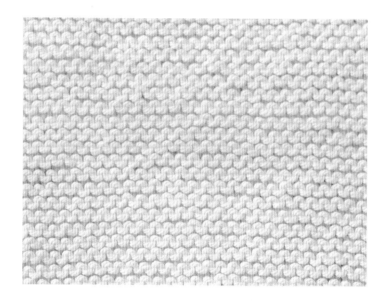

Garter stitch

Ideal for beginners, garter stitch is the simplest of them all. However, take care with it as it can show up inconsistencies in your knitting. Garter stitch is seen at its best when worked in a natural fibre, particularly pure wool, and over fairly small areas, such as in a baby garment. It makes a good detail used on collars and edgings. It can take a little longer to knit up than stocking stitch, though, because two rows of garter stitch only show as one.

Stitch pattern for garter stitch

Cast on any number of stitches.
Knit every row.

Stocking stitch

Stocking stitch is the basis of most knitwear and can be used to create the simplest of garments. It makes an excellent background to show shaping details or embellishments. The knit rows on stocking stitch are considered to be the right side of the fabric and the purl rows, the wrong side.

Stitch pattern for stocking stitch

Cast on any number of stitches.

1st row (right side) Knit.

2nd row (wrong side) Purl.

Repeat the 1st and 2nd rows to form stocking stitch.

Reverse stocking stitch

Reverse stocking stitch fabric is the reverse side of stocking stitch. It is usually used as a background on which cables are worked, as it makes the stocking stitch cables stand out more clearly. I prefer to see it only used in small areas, since it can make the fabric look rather bare and uninteresting.

Stitch pattern for reverse stocking stitch

Cast on any number of stitches.

1st row (right side) Purl.

2nd row (wrong side) Knit.

Repeat the 1st and 2nd rows to form reverse stocking stitch.

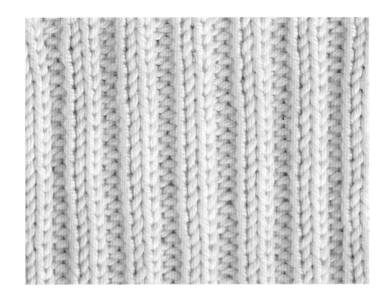

Double ribbing

Ribbings are usually worked as lower borders or neckbands on garments. By pulling the fabric in, ribs prevent garments from fluting at the lower edge and ensure that cuffs fit snugly around the wrist. My own favourite is the '2 by 2' or 'double' rib – it is simple, but I feel is more distinctive than the single rib.

Stitch pattern for double ribbing

Cast on a multiple of 4 stitches, plus 2 extra.

1st row K2, *p2, k2; repeat from * to end.

2nd row P2, *k2, p2; repeat from * to end.

Repeat the 1st and 2nd rows to form double rib.

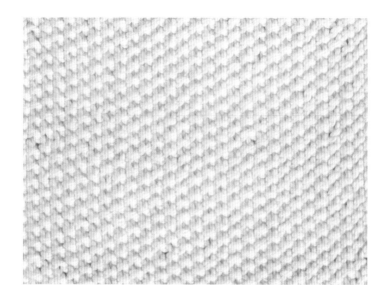

Moss (seed) stitch

Moss stitch is my favourite of all of the simple stitch patterns. It is perfect not only worked as an all-over pattern on a garment, but also as detailing on collars, lower borders and front bands. It makes a beautiful alternative to ribbing. Moss stitch does not knit up as quickly as some patterns because the yarn is being constantly carried back and forth between the front and the back of the work.

Stitch pattern for moss stitch

Cast on an uneven number of stitches.

1st row K1, *p1, k1; repeat from * to end.

Repeat this row to form moss stitch.

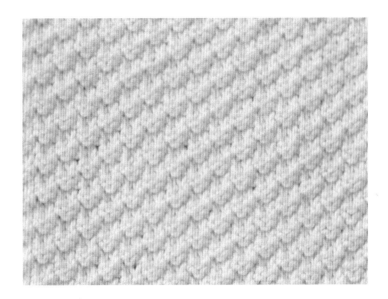

Double moss stitch

Based on single moss stitch, double moss stitch is worked over double the amount of stitches and rows. This creates a more textured, raised effect, which works particularly well as a selvedge on Aran designs.

Stitch pattern for double moss stitch

Cast on a multiple of 4 stitches, plus 2 extra.

1st row K2, *p2, k2; repeat from * to end.

2nd row P2, *k2, p2; repeat from * to end.

3rd row P2, *k2, p2; repeat from * to end.

4th row K2, *p2, k2; repeat from * to end.

Repeat 1st to 4th rows to form moss stitch.

cables

Knitted cables are formed by crossing one set of stitches over another. This is done by leaving stitches on a cable needle at the back of the knitting (creating a cable that crosses to the right) or at the front of the knitting (creating a cable that crosses to the left). A cable needle is a short, double-pointed needle. The cable needles I prefer to work with have a curve in the middle to prevent the stitches from falling off. The cable examples that follow are worked over six stitches, but cables can be worked over a smaller or larger amount of stitches.

- The basic technique is very simple; even the most intricate cables are based on the crossing of stitches.

- There are two types of cable: vertical cables, where they are repeated in a vertical panel across the background, and travelling cables (see opposite), where they move outwards or inwards on the background to form chevrons or diamond shapes.

- As the stitches are pulled away to the left or right, away from the adjacent stitch, a slight ladder can be formed. This can't really be helped as it is the nature of the stitch, but will show less in a wool or wool mix, which has a natural elasticity.

- It is easier to count the rows on the reverse side of a cabled fabric.

- When shaping is required in a pattern where there are all-over cables, as when working a sleeve, for example, it can be neater to continue the cable without crossing for a time at the outer edge.

- When a pattern with cables is worked in measurement rather than rows, work the neck or shoulder shaping a few rows after the last cross so that the piece is finished neatly.

- For best results, use a cable needle that is slightly smaller than the main needles so that the stitches do not stretch.

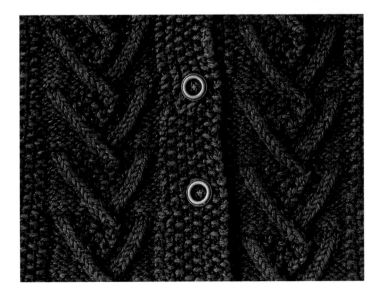

Back cross cable

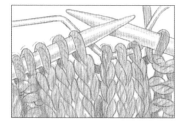

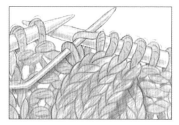

1 Slip the first three cable stitches purlwise off the left-hand needle and onto the cable needle. Leave the cable needle at the back of the work, then knit the next three stitches on the left-hand needle, keeping the yarn tight to prevent a gap from forming in the knitting.

2 Knit the three stitches directly from the cable needle or, if preferred, slip the three stitches from the cable needle back onto the left-hand needle and then knit them. This completes the cable cross.

Front cross cable

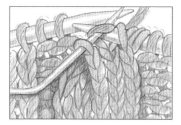

1 Slip the first three cable stitches purlwise off the left-hand needle and onto the cable needle. Leave the cable needle at the front of the work, then knit the next three stitches on the left-hand needle, keeping the yarn tight to prevent a gap from forming in the knitting.

2 Knit the three stitches directly from the cable needle or, if preferred, slip the three stitches from the cable needle back onto the left-hand needle and then knit them. This completes the cable cross.

bobbles

A bobble is created by working increases into one stitch and then reducing them back to one stitch once it is completed. Two versions are shown here — one worked over one row (below) and the other over several turning rows (see page 91). Both can be made bigger or smaller by working fewer or more stitches, or fewer or more rows.

- Although these bobbles are shown worked on a stocking stitch background, you could also work them on reverse stocking stitch.

One-row bobble

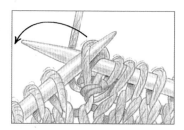 

1 To make four bobble stitches from one stitch, knit into the front of the next stitch in the usual way, then knit into the back, the front and the back of the same stitch before slipping it off the left-hand needle (see 'inc one' on page 96 for how this is done). Lift the second stitch on the right-hand needle over the first stitch and off the needle, as shown.

2 Then take the third and fourth stitches over the first stitch and off the needle in the same way, one at a time. This decreases the four stitches back to the one stitch and completes the one-row bobble.

Multi-row bobble

The multi-row bobble can be worked in either stocking stitch (as it is here) or in reverse stocking stitch, for a different texture. To do this, work your first row after the first turning (step 2) as a knit or a purl row. A multi-row bobble is usually described in a pattern as 'make bobble'.

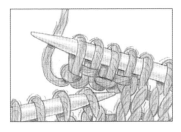

1 To make five bobble stitches from one stitch, knit into the front of the next stitch in the usual way, then knit into the back, the front, the back and the front of the same stitch before slipping it off the left-hand needle (see 'inc one' on page 96 for how this is done).

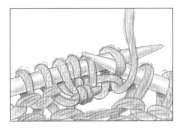

2 Turn your knitting and purl the five bobble stitches, then turn and knit the five stitches. Work one more purl row and one more knit row on these same stitches, so your last row is a right-side row.

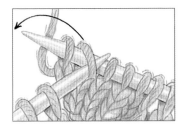

3 With the right side still facing, insert the point of the left-hand needle in the second stitch on the right-hand needle and take it over the first stitch and off the needle. Then do the same with the third, fourth and fifth stitches, one at a time, to complete the bobble.

INCREASING
AND DECREASING

To shape your knitting – for example, along armhole, neck and sleeve edges – there are various techniques you can use to increase or decrease the number of stitches on your needle. The simplest, most frequently used increases and decreases are given on the following pages. Increases and decreases are also used to create lace patterns.

increases

Increases are worked to make your knitted fabric wider by adding to the number of stitches. They are most often used when shaping sleeves or after completing ribbing on the lower edges of backs, fronts and sleeves.

- Increases can be used decoratively to add detailing to an otherwise plain design. Decorative increases like this are placed two or three stitches from the edge of the knitting so that they can be seen after the garment has been sewn up.

- Increasing when working stocking stitch is relatively simple, but when working more complex stitch patterns, check to see if your instructions tell you to work extra increased stitches into the pattern.

- Yarn over increases (see pages 98–9) are usually worked in lace patterns, followed by a decrease to create a hole or eyelet.

Increase 1 ('inc 1')

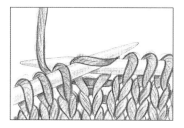

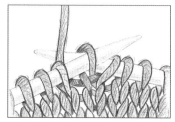

1 Insert the right-hand needle into the front of the next stitch, then knit the stitch but leave it on the left-hand needle.

2 Insert the right-hand needle into the back of the same stitch and knit it. Then slip the original stitch off the needle. You now have an extra stitch on the right-hand needle.

Make 1 ('m1')

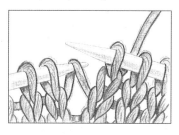

1 Insert the left-hand needle from front to back under the horizontal strand between the stitch just worked on the right-hand needle and the first stitch on the left-hand needle.

2 Knit into the back of the loop to twist it, thus preventing a hole. Then drop the strand from the left-hand needle. This forms a new stitch on the right-hand needle.

Yarn over between knit stitches ('yf')

Bring the yarn forward between the two needles, from the back to the front of the work. Taking the yarn over the needle to do so, knit the next stitch.

Yarn over between a knit and a purl ('yrn')

Bring the yarn forward between the two needles from the back to the front of the work, take it over the top of the needle to the back again, then forward between the needles. Purl the next stitch.

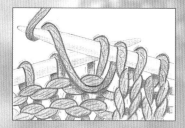

Yarn over between purl stitches ('yrn')

Bring the yarn over the needle to the back, then between the two needles to the front. Then purl the next stitch.

Yarn over between a purl and a knit ('yon')

Take the yarn from the front over the needle to the back. Then knit the next stitch.

decreases

Decreases are used to make your fabric narrower by reducing the number of stitches. They are most often used when shaping necklines or the tops of sleeves.

- As with increases, decreases can form decorative detailing a few stitches from the edge, where different techniques are used to make the decreases slant to the right or left. This type of shaping, called 'fully fashioned', can be useful when shaping necks. By working 'knit 2 together' on the right neck edge and 'slip 1, knit 1, pass slipped stitch over' on the left side a neater edge is created, making it is easier to pick up stitches around the neck for the neckband or collar.

- Worked two stitches in from the neckline edge, the slanting stitches can provide an interesting detail around the neck.

Knit 2 together ('k2tog' or 'dec 1')

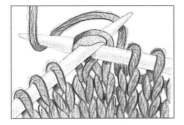

On a knit row, insert the right-hand needle from left to right through the next two stitches on the left-hand needle and knit them together. One stitch has been decreased.

Purl 2 together ('p2tog' or 'dec 1')

On a purl row, insert the right-hand needle from right to left through next two stitches on the left-hand needle. Then purl them together. One stitch has been decreased.

Slip 1, knit 1, pass slipped stitch over ('psso')

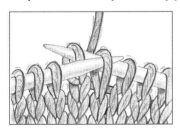

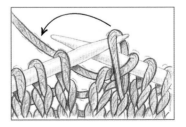

1 Insert the right-hand needle into the next stitch and slip onto the right-hand needle. Knit the next stitch. Insert left-hand needle into the slipped stitch.

2 With the left-hand needle, lift the slipped stitch over the knitted stitch, as shown, and off the right-hand needle.

edgings on knitting

The interesting shapes of knitted edgings are formed using the basic techniques of increasing and decreasing. Yarn overs create the lacy eyelets (see page 104 for how to make eyelets). This selection of edging patterns includes some worked vertically and some worked horizontally. Eyelet daisy edging, narrow lace edging, bobble and lace edging and faggoting with zigzag are knitted as strips that are sewn onto the finished knitting, while scalloped bobble edge and chevron lace can be worked directly onto your knitting. Small picot edge is a simple decorative cast off. All are easy to work and make good exercises for practising edgings.

- Lace edgings are also a great way to tackle lace techniques. Lace can be difficult to grapple with when you are also dealing with shapings for sleeves or armholes. Worked over a small amount of stitches, the first three edgings on the following pages are a perfect way to introduce yourself to all you need to know when you come to knit more complex lace stitch patterns.

Eyelet daisy edging

Cast on 12 sts.

1st row (RS) K1, yf, k2tog, k6, yf, k2tog, k1.

2nd row k12.

3rd row K1, yf, k2, k2tog, yrn twice, k2tog, k2, yf, k2tog, k1.

4th row K7, yf, k2tog, k4.

5th row K1, yf, k1, k2tog, yrn twice, k2tog twice, yrn twice, k2tog, yf, k2tog, k1.

6th row K5, yf, k2tog, k2, yf, k2tog, k3.

7th row K1, yf, k4, k2tog, yrn twice, k2tog, k2, yf, k2tog, k1.

8th row K7, yf, k2tog, k6.

9th row K1, yf, k3tog, k2tog, yrn twice, k2tog twice, yrn twice, k2tog, yf, k2tog, k1.

10th row As 6th row.

11th row K1, yf, k3tog, k1, k2tog, yrn twice, k2tog, k2, yf, k2tog, k1.

12th row As 4th row.

13th row K1, yf, k3tog, k6, yf, k2tog, k1.

14th row K12.

These 14 rows form the patt and are repeated throughout.

Narrow lace edging

Cast on 6 sts.

1st row (RS) K1, k2tog, yf, k2, yrn twice to make a double yarn over, k1.

2nd row K1, k1 and k1tbl both into double yarn over, k2tog, yf, k3.

3rd row K1, k2tog, yf, k5.

4th row Cast off 2 sts, then k2tog, yf, k3.

These 4 rows form the patt and are repeated throughout.

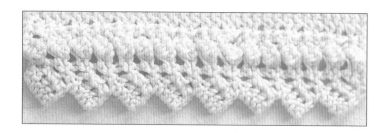

Bobble and lace edging

Cast on 12 sts.

1st row (WS) K4, yf, sl 1, k2tog, psso, yf, k3, yf, k2.

2nd row K4, [k1, p1] 3 times all in next st, p2, k6.

3rd row K4, yf, skpo, k2tog, cast off 5 sts, k2, yf, k2.

4th row K5, yf, k1, p1, k6.

5th row K4, yf, sl 1, k2tog, psso, yf, k3, yf, k2tog, yf, k2.

6th row K6, [k1, p1] 3 times all in next st, p2, k6.

7th row K4, yf, skpo, k2tog, cast off 5 sts, k2, yf, k2tog, yf, k2.

8th row Cast off 4 sts, k2, yf, k1, p1, k6.

These 8 rows form the patt and are repeated throughout.

Scalloped bobble edging

Worked over a multiple of 10 sts, plus 1 extra.

1st row (WS) K to end.

2nd row K5, [k1, p1, k1, p1, k1] all in next st, [turn, k5, turn, p5] twice, then pass 2nd, 3rd, 4th and 5th sts over first st – called *make bobble* or *mb* –, *k9, mb; rep from * to last 5 sts, k5.

3rd and 4th rows K to end.

5th row P1, *yrn, p3, p3tog tbl, p3, yrn, p1; rep from * to end.

6th row K2, *yf, k2, sl 1, k2tog, psso, k2, yf, k3; rep from * to last 9 sts, yf, k2, sl 1, k2tog, psso, k2, yf, k2.

7th row P3, *yrn, p1, p3tog tbl, p1, yrn; p5; rep from * to last 8 sts, yrn, p1, p3tog tbl, p1, yrn, p3.

8th row K4, *yf, sl 1, k2tog, psso, yf, k7; rep from * to last 7 sts, yf, sl 1, k2tog, psso, k4.

9th row P to end.

10th–13th rows K to end. Cast off or, if desired, beg main piece of knitting.

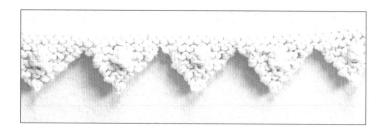

Triangle bobble edging

Worked over a multiple of 9 sts.

1st row (WS) K to end.

2nd and 3rd rows K to end.

**4th row (RS) K9, turn (cont to work on these sts only for 5th–11th rows).

5th row K2tog tbl, k5, k2tog.

6th row K3, [K1, p1, k1, p1, k1, p1, k1] all in next st, then pass 2nd, 3rd, 4th, 5th, 6th and 7th sts over first st, k3.

7th row K2tog tbl, k3, k2tog.

8th row K5.

9th row K2tog tbl, k1, k2tog.

10th row k3.

11th row St 1, k2tog, psso. Fasten off.

With RS facing, rejoin yarn to rem sts.**

Rep from ** to ** until all sts have been worked.

Cast off or, if desired, beg main piece of knitting.

Alternative version: Work in moss stitch or leave off the bobbles.

This edging is worked from a cast-on edge. It can be picked up and knitted down from the hem, but lies flatter if sewn on afterwards.

Small picot edging

Worked over an odd number of sts on the cast-off row.

Cast off row (RS) Cast off one st knitwise, *slip st used in casting off back onto left-hand needle, cast on 2 sts knitwise, cast off 4 sts knitwise; rep from * to end.

Fasten off.

Alternative version: To make the edging more delicate, try casting off 6 sts (see Floral Cardigan on page 81).

Faggoting with zigzag

Cast on 8 sts, K one row.

1st row Sl 1, k1, [yf, k2tog] twice, yf, k2.

2nd row K2, yf, k2, [yf, k2tog] twice, k1.

3rd row Sl 1, k1, [yf, k2tog] twice, k2, yf, k2.

4th row K2, yf, k4, [yf, k2tog] twice, k1.

5th row Sl 1, k1, [yf, k2tog] twice, k4, yf, k2.

6th row K2, yf, k6, [yf, k2tog] twice, k1.

7th row Sl 1, k1, [yf, k2tog] twice, k6, yf, k2.

8th row K2, yf, k8, [yf, k2tog] twice, k1.

9th row Sl 1, k1, [yf, k2tog] twice, k8, yf, k2.

10th row K2, yf, k10, [yf, k2tog] twice, k1.

11th row Sl 1, k1, [yf, k2tog] twice, k10, yf, k2.

12th row Cast off 11 sts, k2, [yf, k2tog] twice, k1.

These 12 rows form the patt and are repeated throughout.

Chevron lace

Worked over a multiple 16 sts, plus 17 extra.

1st row (RS) Skpo, *p2, k2, p2, yon, k1, ym, p2, k2, p2, yb, insert right-hand needle knitwise into 2nd st then first st on left-hand needle and slip these 2 sts, k1, then pass 2 slipped sts over—called *slip 2, knit one, pass slipped stitches over or s2kpsso*—; rep from* to last 15 sts, p2, k2, p2, yon, k1, ym, p2, k2, p2, k2tog.

2nd row P1, *k2, p2, k2, p3, k2, p2, k2, p1; rep from * to end.

3rd row Skpo, *p1, k2, p2, k1, [yf, k1] twice, p2, k2, p1, yb, s2kpsso; rep from * to last 15 sts, p1, k2, p2, k1, [yf, k1] twice, p2, k2, p1, k2tog.

4th row P1, *k1, p2, k2, p5, k2, p2, k1, p1; rep from * to end.

5th row Skpo, *k2, p2, k2, yf, k1, yf, k2, p2, k2, s2kpsso; rep from * to last 15 sts, k2, p2, k2, yf, k1, yf, k2, p2, k2, k2tog.

6th row P3, *k2, p7, k2, p5; rep from * to last 14 sts, k2, p7, k2, p3.

7th row Skpo, *k1, p2, k2, p1, yon, k1, ym, p1, k2, p2, k1, s2kpsso; rep from * to last 15 sts, k1, p2, k2, p1, yon, k1, ym, p1, k2, p2, k1, k2tog.

8th row P2, *k2, p2, k1, p3, k1, p2, k2, p3; rep from * to last 15 sts, k2, p2, k1, p3, k1, p2, k2, p2.

Cast off or, if desired, beg main piece of knitting.

edging tips

The edgings given on the previous two pages would all make beautiful additions to a knitted garment, blanket or cushion. The trick is to marry the right edging with the right main stitch texture.

- Take care when working some knitted edgings. As on lace patterns, even when worked over a relatively small amount of stitches, the edging rows with their yarn overs and working stitches together can be quite treacherous. Check that you have the right amount of stitches at the end of each row.

- Most edgings are best worked in a finer yarn, particularly cotton, for crisp stitch detailing.

- Ideas for edgings can sometimes be informed by the pattern on the main part of the knit you are designing – such as matching a particular stitch pattern like moss stitch or garter stitch – but sometimes inspiration can come from seeing an eyelet edging on a beautiful linen pillowcase, or a broderie anglaise border on a crisp cotton tablecloth.

FIXING MISTAKES

Even the most experienced knitter makes mistakes, and for the beginner they can actually be a way of learning more about how the fabric is constructed. Most errors are easily converted, and the following pages show you how to fix the most common ones.

picking up dropped stitches

A dropped or incorrect stitch is a common mistake. Depending on the type of stitch dropped or when the mistake occurred, you can pick up, unpick or unravel using the methods introduced here and overleaf.

Picking up a knit stitch on the row below

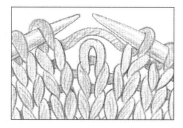

1 Pick up the dropped stitch as soon as possible or it will continue to drop further down the work.

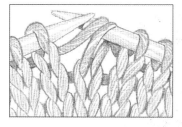

2 Working from front to back, pick up the stitch and the horizontal strand above it with the right-hand needle (the strand should be behind the stitch).

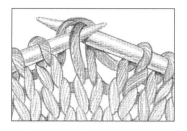

3 Insert the left-hand needle through the back of the stitch and lift it over the strand and off the needle as though casting off (see page 75).

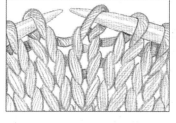

4 The stitch is made facing the wrong way. To right it, insert the left-hand needle through the front of the stitch and slip it onto the needle.

Picking up a purl stitch on the row below

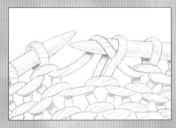

1 Pick up the dropped stitch as soon as possible or it will continue to drop further down the work.

2 With the strand in front of the stitch and working from back to front, pick up the stitch and the horizontal strand above it with the right-hand needle.

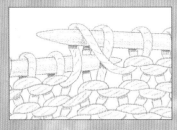

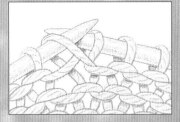

3 Insert the left-hand needle behind the strand and through the stitch. Now lift the stitch.

4 With the right-hand needle, draw the strand through the lifted stitch, so forming a stitch on the right-hand needle.

- If more than one stitch has been dropped, secure the others with a safety pin until you are ready to pick them up.

Picking up a stitch several rows below

The dropped stitch forms a ladder running down a number of rows. Using a crochet hook and working from the front of the fabric, insert the hook into the free stitch. With the hook pointing upwards, catch the first strand of the ladder from above and draw it through the stitch. Repeat until all the strands have been worked, then replace the stitch on the left-hand needle.

unravelling a mistake

To go back stitch-by-stitch when a mistake has occurred more than a few rows down really is not only time consuming, but also irritating. The quick way is to take the work off the needle and unravel it. Unravel the knitting to the row below the mistake, replace the stitches on the needle (ensuring that you have not twisted them – but if this should happen, see page 122) and continue knitting.

- With some yarns it may be difficult to replace the stitches neatly, so in these instances, unravel to the row above the mistake, replacing the stitches on the needle, and unpick one row, as below.

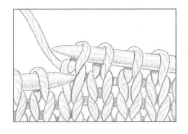

◁ On a knit row

With yarn at the back and the knitting on the right-hand needle, insert the left-hand needle from front to back through the centre of the first stitch below the stitch on the right-hand needle. Withdraw the right-hand needle from the stitch and pull yarn away.

▷ On a purl row

Unpick a purl row in the same way as on a knit row, but with the yarn at the front of the work.

untwisting stitches

A 'twisted' stitch is formed by dropping a stitch and replacing it on the needle backwards or by incorrectly wrapping the yarn on the previous row. Twisted stiches are easily recognisable and simple to correct.

On a knit row

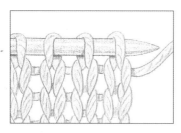

1 The third stitch on the needle has been twisted.

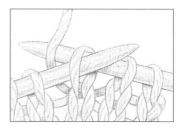

2 To correct the twisted stitch, knit it through the back of the loop.

On a purl row

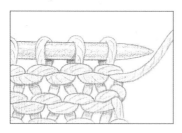

1 The third stitch on the needle has been twisted.

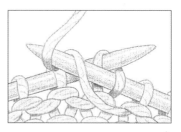

2 To correct the twisted stitch, purl it through the back of the loop.

COLOUR KNITTING

Colour knitting covers a range of techniques, and you will need to choose the one that suits the type of colour knitting you are working on. The three basic techniques are stranding yarns, weaving in yarns and intarsia knitting. If you want to learn the techniques from scratch or just brush up on them, follow the step-by-step instructions in this section. My special tips for colour knitting are given on pages 142–5.

stranding

Stranding is used when colours are worked over a small amount of stitches, usually a maximum of four. The yarns are picked up over and under one another, which prevents them from tangling. It is the technique used for the small repeats in Fair Isle patterns, where only two colours are used in a single row.

- All you have to do when stranding is leave the colour you are not knitting with hanging on the wrong side of the knitting and pick it up again when you need it. This creates loose strands or 'floats' on the wrong side.

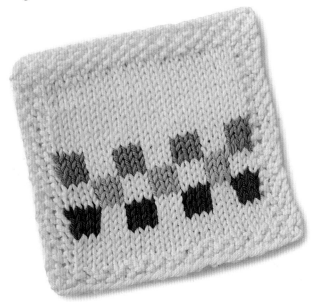

Stranding on a knit row

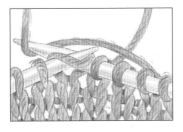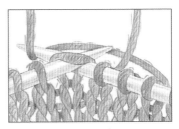

1 On a right-side (knit) row, to change colours drop the colour you were using. Then pick up the new colour, take it *over* the top of the dropped colour and start knitting with it.

2 To change back to the old colour, drop the colour you were knitting with. Then pick up the old colour, take it *under* the dropped colour and knit to the next colour change, and so on.

Stranding on a purl row

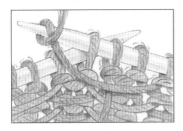

1 On a wrong-side (purl) row, to change colours drop the colour you were using. Then pick up the new colour, take it *over* the top of the dropped colour and start purling with it.

2 To change back to the old colour, drop the colour you were knitting with. Then pick up the old colour, take it *under* the dropped colour and purl to the next colour change, and so on.

stranding tips

The stranding technique is used when each colour is only used over a few – usually less than four – stitches.

- To practise stranding, try knitting a simple checkerboard pattern. First, cast on a multiple of stitches divisible by three, plus any stitches you wish to work as your border on either side (see page 126).

- Before starting the colour pattern, work your lower border in a single colour. Then, on the first colourwork row, work three stitches in your contrast colour and three stitches in your main colour alternately along the row, using the techniques shown on page 127 to avoid twisting and tangling your yarns. Work four rows like this, then alternate the colours to create the checkerboard effect.

- Try to make sure that you are feeling fairly calm – anxiety is bound to make your knitting tighter! Your aim is to keep your knitting relaxed so that you do not pull the yarn too tightly across the back of the work. Keep a good, even tension and smooth your stitches out on the needle; if you do this, your colour knitting will lie as flat as stocking stitch in a single colour and will have the same amount of give.

- To make the exercise less monotonous, use other contrast colours on your pattern. I like to pat and 'tweak' my knitting when working in colour. Handling the knitted fabric can sometimes smooth out small inconsistencies, and you will be able to tell if your knitting is becoming too tight by how the stitches slip along the needle.

- On completion of your swatch, press it lightly and check to make sure that the fabric has not pulled in over the colourwork.

- If you haven't used them already, try bamboo needles – their silky finish makes them perfect for colour knitting.

- A checkerboard is a useful colour design to master. It can look good as a gingham, with one contrast shade a deeper tone than the other. Checks work really well when contrasted with other patterns such as florals or Fair Isles.

weaving in

When there are more than four stitches between colour changes, long floats at the back of the work can make the knitted fabric too inflexible. These long floats can also catch on fingers, particularly on the inside of sleeves, which is especially inconvenient on children's garments. This is when the 'weaving in' technique, where the floats are caught into the back of the stitches, is used.

Weaving in on a knit row

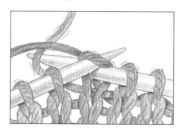

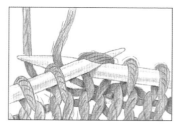

1 To weave yarn on a knit row, insert the right-hand needle into the next stitch and lay the yarn to be woven in over the right-hand needle. Knit the stitch with the working yarn, taking it under the yarn not in use and making sure you do not catch this strand into the knitted stitch.

2 Knit the next 2 or 3 stitches with the working yarn, taking it over the yarn being woven in. Continue like this, weaving the loose colour over and under the working yarn alternately with every 3rd or 4th stitch until you need to use it again.

Weaving in on a purl row

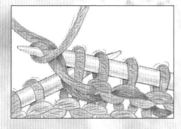 

1 To weave yarn on a purl row, insert the right-hand needle into the next stitch and lay the yarn to be woven in over the right-hand needle. Purl the stitch with the working yarn, taking it under the yarn not in use and making sure you do not catch this strand into the purled stitch.

2 Purl the next 2 or 3 stitches with the working yarn, taking it over the yarn being woven in. Continue like this, weaving the loose colour over and under the working yarn alternately with every 3rd or 4th stitch until you need to use it again.

weaving in tips

For a weaving-in swatch, cast on a multiple of six stitches plus one extra, plus your border stitches.

- On your first colour row, work one stitch in the contrast colour and five stitches in the main colour alternately along the row. Weave in on the middle stitch in the main shade between the stitches in the contrast colour using the technique shown on page 132. Continue to work the chevron pattern as shown on the swatch opposite below.

- This small chevron pattern is ideal for practising this technique, as you only need to weave in on the first row (a right-side row) and the last row (a wrong-side row). This demonstrates that often on Fair Isles you only need to use the technique as and when required.

- Don't weave in on alternate stitches, as this makes the fabric too rigid, and the contrast colour will show through. In some small Fair Isle patterns you may only need to use stranding, in others a combination of stranding and weaving in.

- If you are weaving in a yarn on the wrong side of your knitting, it is best to avoid any very strong contrasts in colour, as the woven-in yarn may show through to the other side. It looks particularly unattractive when a very dark shade can be seen behind the stitches of a far lighter shade.

intarsia motifs

Intarsia is used when blocks of colour are being worked in separate areas of the knitted fabric. For these types of designs, there is no need to carry the colour (or colours) used for the motif across the entire row of knitting. Also, weaving in or stranding yarns would make the fabric too rigid, and it would look messy on the right side. By using a separate ball (or balls) of yarn for each area of colour and twisting the yarns together where they meet, the fabric will look neat and lie flat. This is called the 'intarsia' technique.

Changing colours on a vertical line

If the two colour areas are forming a vertical line, to change colours on a knit row drop the colour you were using. Pick up the new colour and wrap it around the dropped colour, as shown, then continue with the new colour. Twist the yarns together on knit and purl rows in this same way at vertical-line colour changes.

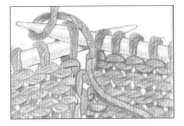

Changing colours on a right diagonal

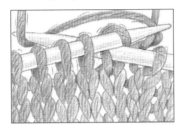

If the two colour areas are forming a right diagonal line, on a knit row drop the colour you were using. Pick up the new colour and wrap it around the dropped colour, as shown, then continue with the new colour. Twist the yarns together on knit rows only at right-diagonal colour changes.

Changing colours on a left diagonal

If the two colour areas are forming a left diagonal line, on a purl row drop the colour you were using. Pick up the new colour and wrap it around the colour you just dropped, as shown, then continue with the new colour. Twist the yarns together on purl rows only at left-diagonal colour changes.

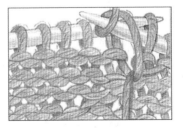

intarsia tips

The intarsia technique is used when individual blocks of colour are worked. This can mean that on some motif knitting you may have to work with a lot of separate lengths of yarn across a row. Do not be tempted to avoid this by using the stranding or weaving-in techniques – your motifs won't lie flat, and the main background colour may well show through.

- The best way to try out intarsia is to knit a swatch where two colours are divided vertically, using the techniques on page 137 which show how to twist the main colour and contrast colour to avoid holes.

- You will notice a slight difference in size between the stitch at the colour change in one row and the one above. It is difficult to achieve the perfect match, but it can help to try to maintain the same tension on every row. At its worst, the looser stitch will bulge out as it is squeezed by the tighter stitch on the row above. Some discrepancies will often even out when the piece is washed.

- The floral swatch on page 136 is an example of using small amounts of separate strands of colour when working small motifs. Afterwards, these ends are darned in on the back, following the lines of the colour change so they do not show through to the other side.

- Try using medium lengths of yarn for each colour in your intarsia rather than using bobbins or small balls. The yarns are bound to tangle, and lengths of yarn can be pulled through if the colours do twist together.

working from a chart

Colour designs for knitting are usually given as a chart on a squared graph. Each square on the chart represents a stitch and each horizontal row of squares represents a row of knitting. The colours are shown on the chart either as actual colours or as symbols.

- Just as you knit starting at the bottom of your knitting and working upwards, so you read the chart – from the bottom row upwards to the top row. Unless stated otherwise, the first row of the knitting chart represents the first row of the knitting, and it is followed from right to left and worked in knit stitches.

- The second row of the chart represents the second row of knitting, which is a purl row, and it is read from left to right.

- If the colour pattern is a repeated design, the chart will indicate how many stitches are in each repeat. The stitches before and after the repeat are the 'edge stitches'. You knit the edge stitches at the beginning of the row, then knit the 'repeat' as many times as necessary until you reach the edge stitches at the end of the row.

- The number of rows in the pattern repeat is usually as many rows as there are on the chart.

colour knitting tips

Many knitters are put off by colour knitting because they think it is more difficult than it really is. One or two bad experiences mean that they avoid it in the future because they feel they are not proficient enough to tackle it. In reality, colour knitting is simple as long as you know which technique is appropriate for a particular type of colourwork.

- Make practice swatches, which take you through all the colour techniques that you need to know – stranding, weaving in and intarsia. For your first attempts, use wool as it gives a neater appearance – being a more 'forgiving' yarn with fibres that draw the stitches together.

- If you do use cotton, remember that poor-quality, or stringy, cotton can make colourwork look less tidy than when it is worked in a better-quality one.

- I like to work a border of garter stitch or moss stitch around my colour samples. It makes them look neater, and if you have a border, you don't have to sew in the yarn ends at the selvedges.

- Keep your test swatches, even if you feel they don't work, because they are often useful for reference later on – if only to remind yourself not to go down that particular colour route again!

combining colours

The Fair Isle swatch opposite is a good example of how effective the simplest of Fair Isles can be. Any Fair Isle, however small, has enormous possibilities.

- Choose a colour pattern from a Fair Isle chart and see how many variations you can achieve. By using a thicker weight yarn, or by using bold colours on a dark background and pastel shades on a light background, you can see the endless variations that you can get out of just one pattern.

- Working in this way can also demonstrate just how hard using colour can be. Shades that look wonderful in the ball before you start knitting can look disappointing when knitted up. This is often due to the proportion you use of each colour. A strong shade can overpower a softer one, or a subtle dusky shade can look dirty when put against a brighter one. It sometimes takes me four or five attempts before I find a colourway that I am happy with.

- If there are one or two rows that you feel don't work, try Swiss darning or duplicate stitch over them in other colours to see if they work better (see page 170).

- The floral motif shown on page 136 would look equally good worked using rich colours against a dark background, or using tones of one colour, such as dark and light blues, for the flower and leaves.

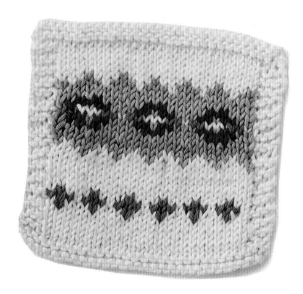

- There are fantastic colour ranges available from the manufacturers now. It can sometimes be as overwhelming as it is exciting when confronted in a yarn store by all the possibilities that are available to you. I find it helpful to keep a file of favourite postcards, images torn from magazines, and printed fabrics that all have interesting colourways that I would not have necessarily come up with myself. They can often provide the stimulus to create your own colour combinations.

- If you want to experiment with different combinations, but don't necessarily want to buy a ball of yarn for each shade, buy small amounts of tapestry thread of those shades. This can also be used to Swiss darn (see page 170) over a portion of your colourwork that you may not feel works.

SEAMS

The making up of a garment and adding of picked up borders is the last, but one of the most important, stages in producing a professional-looking garment. A beautifully knitted garment can be ruined by careless sewing up or unevenly picked up borders, as the knitter hurries to complete the project. Here are the basic techniques for helping you perfect those finishing touches.

seam basics

The seam that I use for almost all sewing up is mattress stitch, which produces a wonderful invisible seam (see pge 155). It works well on any yarn, and makes a completely straight seam, as the same amount is taken up on each side. This also means that the knitted pieces should not need to be pinned together first. I find mattress stitch particularly invaluable when sewing seams on Fair-Isle bands or striped pieces of knitting.

- When sewing up a garment worked in a textured yarn, use a smooth yarn. In mattress stitch the seam is invisible, so even a contrast shade won't show.

- The seam for joining two cast-off edges is handy for shoulder seams, while the seam for joining a cast-off edge with a side edge (selvedge) is usually used when sewing a sleeve onto the body on a dropped shoulder style.

- It is best to leave a long tail at the casting-on stage to sew up your knitting with, so that the sewing up yarn is already secured in place. If this is not possible, when first securing the thread for the seam you should leave a length that can be darned in afterwards.

- All seams on knitting should be sewn with a large, blunt-ended yarn or tapestry needle, to avoid splitting the yarn.

choosing a seam

Y ou can choose to take in one stitch or half a stitch
on your seam. On a thicker yarn it is better to take in half
a stitch, so you don't have too bulky a seam.

Rib seam: joining knit- and purl-stitch edges

Skip the purl stitch at the edge of one piece of knitting and join the seam at the centre of knit stitches, as for joining two knit-stitch edges.

Rib seam: joining two knit-stitch edges

Insert the needle under a horizontal bar in the centre of a knit stitch at the edge of one piece of knitting, then at the edge of the other piece. Continue to do this, drawing up the thread to form one complete knit stitch along the seam.

Beginning a seam

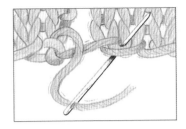

With right sides facing you, thread the tail from your cast-on row into a blunt-ended sewing needle. Insert the needle from back to front through the corner stitch of the other piece. Make a figure of eight and insert the needle back into the original stitch. Pull the thread through to join the two pieces together.

Mattress stitch on stocking stitch

With the right sides of the knitting facing you, insert the needle under the horizontal bar between the first stitch and next stitch. Then insert the needle under the same bar on the other piece. Continue to do this, drawing up the thread to form the seam.

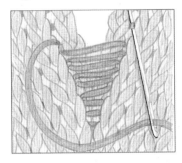

Mattress stitch on garter stitch

With the right sides of the knitting facing you, insert the needle through the bottom of the knot on the edge and then through the top of the corresponding knot on the opposite edge. Continue to do this from edge to edge, drawing up the thread to form a flat seam.

Joining two cast-off edges in stocking stitch

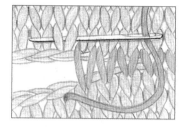 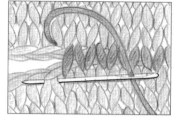

1 With the cast-off edges butted together, bring the needle out in the centre of the first stitch just below the cast-off edge on one piece. Insert the needle through the centre of the first stitch on the other piece and out through the centre of the next stitch.

2 Next, insert the needle through the centre of the first stitch on the first piece again and out through the centre of the stitch next to it. Continue in this way until the seam is completed.

Joining two cast-off edges in garter stitch

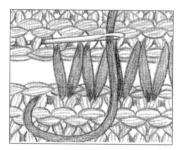

Insert the needle under the two strands of a cast-off stitch on one edge and then under two strands of a cast-off stitch on the other edge. Continue in this way from edge to edge, drawing up the thread to form a flat seam.

Joining a cast-off edge and a selvedge

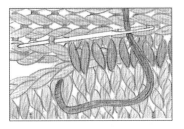

Bring the needle back to the front through the centre of the first stitch on the cast-off edge. Then insert it under one or two horizontal strands between the first and second stitches on the selvedge, and back through the centre of the same cast-off stitch. Continue in this way until the seam is completed.

Joining a cast-off edge and a selvedge in garter stitch

Bring the needle back to the front through the centre of the first stitch on the cast-off edge. Then insert it through the top of the knot on the selvedge, and back through the centre of the same cast-off stitch. Pull up the thread so the seaming stitches disappear. Continue in this way until the seam is completed.

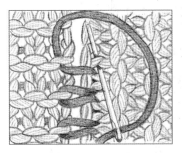

Darning in ends

You will always have some ends to darn in, which can be sewn vertically or horizontally. Thread the loose end onto a blunt-ended needle and run it over and under the horizontal bars of the stitches at the back of the work. Ends can also be darned in vertically along the edge of the pieces after seaming.

knitting in the round

Knitting in the round is the way you can produce seamless knitting. Historically, this is the way that the traditional fisherman's sweaters and Fair Isles were worked, the piece being tubular up to the armholes and then divided to work backwards and forwards.

- Circular needles are used for bigger pieces, as the flexible wire joining the two points can hold many stitches.

- When you join the first row that you have cast on (that is, after you have completed the last stitch and knitted the first stitch that you cast on), make sure the stitches are not twisted around the needle – as this will result in a twisted fabric like a Mobius strip.

- Double-pointed needles are used for smaller pieces such as socks and hats. The stitches are evenly divided between three or four needles and the fourth or fifth used to knit with. As with circular needles, take care not to twist the cast-on row.

- When working tubular knitting, place a marker between the first and last cast-on stitch to help you identify the beginning of each new round.

- There are no purl rows in circular knitting, the right side always faces you.

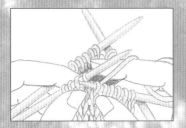

The needles form a triangle or square. Begin by casting on the number of stitches required on one needle and then divide them evenly across the others. Then use the fourth or fifth needle to begin knitting by inserting it into the first cast-on stitch. Continue to work in rounds.

picking up stitches

Picking up stitches' is a technique used when you need to knit a border directly onto a piece of knitting, for instance to add button bands on a cardigan or a neckband along a neck edge. To do this, you draw loops through the knitting with the tip of your knitting needle, forming stitches directly onto your needle.

- Your knitting pattern will tell you how many stitches to pick up, and this should be done evenly. In the pattern, the instruction usually reads 'pick up and knit'.

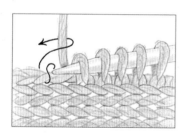

◁ Along a selvedge
With the right side of the knitting facing, insert the knitting needle from front to back between the first and second stitches of the first row. Wrap the yarn around the needle and pull a loop through to form a new stitch on the needle. Continue in this way along the edge of the knitting.

▷ Along a neck edge
On a neck edge, work along the straight edges as for a selvedge. But along the curved edges, insert the needle through the centre of the stitch below the shaping (to avoid large gaps) and pull a loop of yarn through to form a new stitch on the needle.

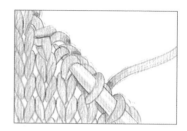

FINISHING TOUCHES

A basic sweater can often be transformed by adding decorative details, such as embroidery or beading. Even an existing garment can be given a fashion update by changing the buttons.

embroidery basics

The knitted fabric is a good base for embroidery, as you can use the vertical and horizontal lines as a guide for where to put your stitches. I have included stitches here that I think look especially good on knitting.

- Make sure you choose your embroidery yarn or thread with care – too thin and it will disappear in the fabric, too thick and it will pull and distort the piece of knitting.

- Use a blunt-ended yarn or tapestry needle.

- Simple motifs or Swiss darning can be worked directly onto the knitting. For more intricate embroidery, draw the pattern onto tissue paper, and then embroider through the paper and the knitted fabric. Pull away the tissue after the embroidery has been completed.

When you start your embroidery, secure the end of the thread on the wrong side of the knitting before beginning the stitch, or leave a long, loose end to darn in later.

Cross stitch

Use the line of the knitted fabric as a guide by working over one, two, or more, knitted stitches and rows. Bring the needle and the thread through and make a diagonal stitch up and to the left. Make a row of diagonal stitches like this from right to left. Then make a return row of diagonal stitches, completing the crosses from left to right as shown below.

 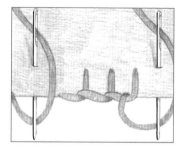

Blanket stitch

Secure the thread at the edge of the knitting. Insert the needle from front to back through the knitting a short distance from the edge, and bring it out below the edge and with the thread under the needle point. Pull the thread through, then insert the needle in the same way, leaving a small gap between the stitches and bringing the needle out again below the edge and with the thread under the needle point. Continue like this along the edge.

French knots

Bring needle and thread through, then wind the thread around the needle twice. Keeping the thread tautly wrapped around the needle, reinsert the needle very near where the thread first emerged and take it through to the back of the knitting. Bring the needle up in the correct position for the next knot.

 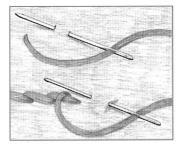

Stem stitch

Bring the needle and the thread through the knitting, then insert the needle at a slight angle, as shown. Pull the needle through, continue making short, slightly angled stitches in this way from left to right.

Satin stitch

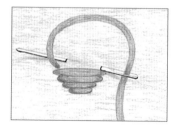

Bring the needle and thread through, then work parallel stitches close together. The stitches can be made straight across or at an angle, depending on the effect desired. Do not pull the thread too tightly or the knitting will become distorted.

Swiss darning or duplicate stitch

Embroidery on knitting can also be in the form of Swiss darning or duplicate stitch, which traces the path of the knit stitches. To prevent colour being swamped by the texture, Swiss darning can be used to provide the colour rather than knitting it in, as it enhances the effect.

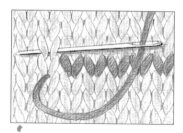

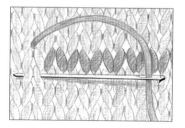

1 Thread a blunt-ended needle with yarn the same weight as the stitch you are darning over. Bring the needle out at the base of the first stitch you want to cover, then take it under the base of the stitch above.

2 Take the needle back through the base of the first stitch and out at the base of the next stitch. Cover each stitch this way.

embroidery tips

Embroidery is one of my favourite ways of enhancing my knitwear. A simple jacket can be transformed by embroidering a collar or pocket; it can brighten up a dull garment or update a classic. I particularly love embroidery when it is used against a very contrasting yarn, or as brights worked on a rustic tweedy yarn.

- Embroidering your knitting can be a good way of adding colour to a garment if you are a fairly novice knitter and do not feel quite ready to tackle large areas of colourwork. On one of my first handknits, I worked tiny embroidered bees on the collar and cuffs of a simple, white baby's cardigan – they provided surprisingly effective details.

- Use embroidery within knitted stitch patterns. I have a cupboard full of old 1940s and 1950s knitting patterns that often include variations on Tyrolean designs, where embroidery is used within the cable patterns.

- Look for inspirational details on old fabrics found in junk shops and car boot or garage sales. A recent trip to Chinatown resulted in me staggering back home with a treasure trove of goodies – embroidered slippers and bags, and a tiny pair of silk shoes for a baby.

- Don't worry about embroidery stitches being perfectly applied. In fact, I think there can be an energy and charm in something that looks homemade – in the best sense of the word. It looks more personal and less mass produced.

buttons and beads

Whether mother-of-pearl, crystal or wood, use buttons and beads to decorate, highlight or add glamour to your handknit designs.

- Detailing with beads can enhance a plain garment and be used simply as an edging, or more elaborately; for example, as an all-over design on an evening bag. You can sew beads onto your finished piece of knitting, or knit them right in.

- When knitting with beads, match the weight of your yarn to the beads you are using. Beads will add weight to your garment and beads that are too heavy on a light yarn will make the garment sag.

- If you want to add beads to a chunky garment and the yarn is too thick to thread through beads, you can always sew them on afterwards.

When you knit with beads, thread the beads onto your yarn before you start knitting. If your yarn is thin enough, you can thread it onto a needle, then pass the needle through the centre of each bead. But if your yarn is too thick to do this, use the technique for threading given on page 177.

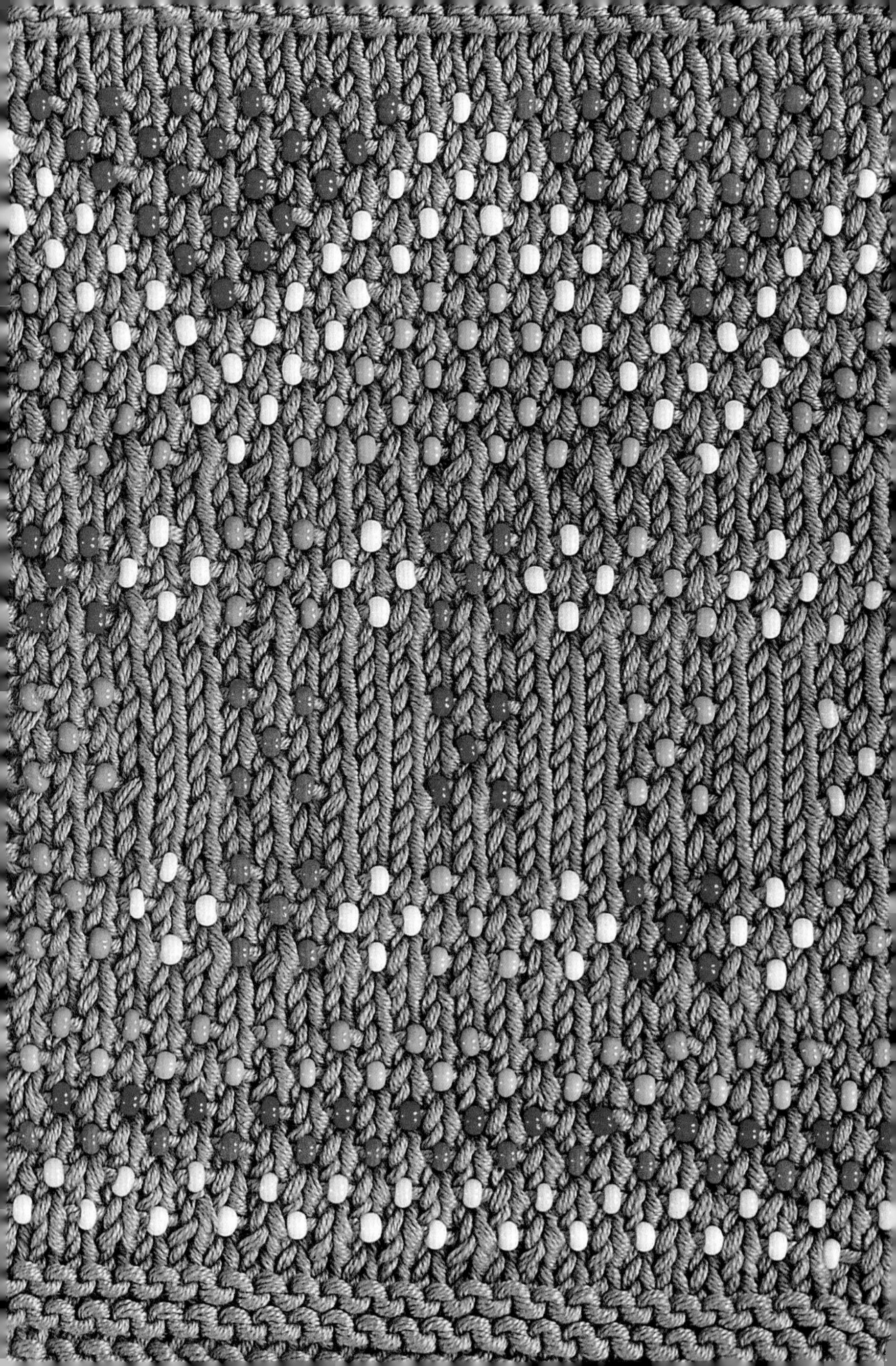

Knitting beads into stocking stitch

The beading method shown here uses a slipped stitch, which means that beads are placed with at least one stitch between them. On the next bead row, the beads are worked so they are staggered between those on the previous bead row – this compensates for the slipped stitches shortening the knitting on the row before.

When threading beads onto a thicker piece of yarn, fold a length of fine but strong sewing thread around the end of your knitting yarn, then thread both ends of the sewing thread through the needle. Pass the needle through the beads and push the beads over the needle and sewing thread and onto the looped yarn, as shown.

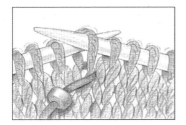

1 On a right-side (knit) row, knit to the position for the bead. Then bring the yarn to the front of the work between the two needles and slip the next stitch purlwise.

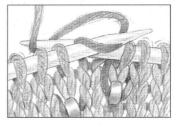

2 Push the bead up close to the front of the knitting. Then take the yarn to the back of the work between the two needles, leaving the bead at the front. Knit the next stitch tightly to keep the bead in place.

beads on knitting

Bead knitting has a great historical tradition, from intricate Victorian beaded purses to neat 1950s' cardigans with beaded borders. It can add an instant touch of glamour to a simple edge on a jacket or make a perfect evening purse.

- There are a variety of shapes and types of beads to work with: round, oval, square or faceted, in glass, metal, wood and ceramic. If your local store does not stock the variety that you need, look around in junk shops, car boot sales or flea markets – you are bound to find an unstrung necklace or two. Better still, if you are really lucky, you may find a beautiful, antique, beaded cardigan or a retro handbag to inspire you.

- You may want to use beads on a sportier design – a chunky jacket, for example. Wooden beads can look great against a heavyweight cotton, or bright primaries on tougher styles, such as biker or denim jackets. (On chunky knits, because of the weight of the yarn, you will probably need to sew the beads on afterwards.)

- Use beads as details to highlight the inside of cables, or use them in geometric or floral patterns.

- Try out your own ideas, starting with easy geometrics, by drawing out patterns on graph paper. Remember that with the beading technique on page 177, you can only bead every alternate stitch and alternate row.

buttons on knitting

Buttons can also be used to add decorative detailing. There are some great styles available now, so make use of them.

- Cheap, tacky buttons can ruin a garment, no matter how good a quality the yarn, but the right buttons can add charm and style.

- Metallic buttons, such as pewter and bronze, can look wonderful on denim-jacket-style designs. My favourite is mother-of-pearl. If I am unsure of the type or colour of button that would suit my design, I know I can rely on mother-of-pearl for quality and to pick up and reflect the shade of the yarn.

- Children love nursery-style buttons and you can involve them by letting them choose their own special ones.

- If a garment of yours outlives its sell-by date, before you throw it out, remember to check the buttons – you can use them again.

- Make sure you sew buttons on garments for babies really securely – small children love to fiddle with them or suck them and could cause them to choke if they come loose or are swallowed.

- Quirky buttons can induce some character into a knit. I particularly like big, bold buttons on jackets and coats.

CARE OF GARMENTS

Taking care of your knitted garments is important. If you have invested all that time and labour into knitting them, you want them to look good for as long as possible. Follow these simple care guidelines for the best results.

Debbie Bliss

washing and drying your knitting

Check the ball band on your yarn for washing instructions. Many yarns can now be machine washed on a delicate wool cycle. You may find it helpful to make a note of the measurements of the garment, such as the width and length, prior to washing. After washing, lay the garment flat and check the measurements again to see if they are the same. If not, smooth and pat the piece of clothing back into shape.

- Natural fibres are usually best hand washed, even if the ball band says otherwise. I find that after successive machine washes, cotton in particular can become rather hard.

- Use soap flakes specially created for hand knits, and warm rather than hot water. Handle the knits gently in the water – do not rub or wring them out, because this can felt the fabric. Rinse well to get rid of any soap, and squeeze out excess water.

- You may need to get rid of more water by rolling the garment in a towel, or you can use the delicate spin cycle of the washing machine. Dry the garment by laying it out flat on top of a towel to absorb moisture, then smooth it and pat into shape. Do not dry knits near sources of direct heat, such as a radiator.

- Store your knits loosely folded to allow the air to circulate.

Index

Acknowledgements

This book would not have been possible without the invaluable contribution of the following people. The knitters, Pat Church, Lynda Clarke, Penny Hill, Shirley Kennet, Maisie Lawrence, Beryl Salter and Frances Wallace. Rosy Tucker for her sharp eye for proofreading. Sandra Lane and Sandra Lousada, for the beautiful photography. Sammie Bell, for her lovely styling and contribution to the concept of the book. Heather Jeeves, a fantastic agent. Imogen Fortes and Emma Callery for being such wonderful editors. The models – a huge thank you to Max, Ceri, Cressy, Istvan, Ciara, Summer, Nell, Thea, Grace, Katie and Natalie.